peace of mind

INSPIRATIONAL QUOTATIONS

Wherever we live, whoever we are, we all desire peace of mind.

The words and images in this book are from many

parts of the world and different kinds of people.

Together, they indicate what may lead to peace of

mind and how it can be fostered.

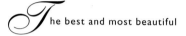he best and most beautiful

things in the world cannot

be seen or even touched.

They must be felt with the heart.

HELEN KELLER

$\mathcal{I}$t is those who have a deep and real inner life who are

best able to deal with the irritating details of outer life.

EVELYN UNDERHILL

True peace of mind comes

from accepting the worst.

LIN YUTANG

$\mathscr{C}$ontentment consists not in adding more fuel, but in taking away some fire: not in multiplying of wealth but in subtracting men's desires.

THOMAS FULLER

*D*ifficult times have helped me to understand better

than before how infinitely rich and beautiful life is in

every way and that so many things that one goes

worrying about are of no importance whatsoever.

ISAK DINESEN

$\mathcal{C}$ontentment comes as the

result of great acceptances

and great humilities,

of surrendering ourselves

to the fullness of life, of

letting life flow through us.

DAVID GRAYSON

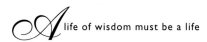 life of wisdom must be a life

of contemplation combined with action.

M. SCOTT PECK

*F*irst keep the peace within

yourself, then you can also bring

peace to others.

THOMAS À KEMPIS

*H*ave courage for the great sorrows of life and

patience for the small ones, and when you have laboriously

accomplished your daily tasks go to sleep in peace.

VICTOR HUGO

If you have a contented mind, you have enough to enjoy life with.

PLAUTUS

I have learned, in whatsoever state I am, therewith to be content.

I've looked over, and I've seen the promised land.

I'm not worried about anything. I'm not fearing any man.

MARTIN LUTHER KING JNR.

$\mathscr{S}$tore up reservoirs of calm

and content and draw on them

at later moments when the

source isn't there, but

the need is very great.

RUPERT BROOKE

$\mathcal{I}$t is a difficult lesson to learn today – to leave one's friends

and family and deliberately practise the art of solitude for an

hour or a day or a week. And yet, once it is done, there is a

quality to being alone that is incredibly precious.

ANNE MORROW LINDBERGH

*O*f one thing I am certain, the body

is not the measure of healing –

peace is the measure.

GEORGE MELTON

*I*f we go down into ourselves

we find that we possess exactly

what we desire.

SIMONE WEIL

*A*ll you need is deep within

you waiting to unfold and

reveal itself. All you have to

do is be still and take time to

seek for what is within, and

you will surely find it.

EILEEN CADDY

It is very strange that the years teach us

patience. The shorter our time, the greater

our capacity for waiting.

ELIZABETH TAYLOR

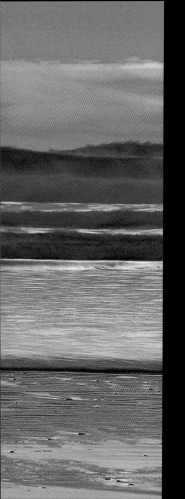

$\mathcal{T}$here is no joy but ca

$\mathscr{T}$he secret of contentment is knowing how

to enjoy what you have, and to be able to

lose all desire for things beyond your reach.

LIN YUTANG

The wise man thinks about his troubles only when there is some

purpose in doing so; at other times he thinks about other things.

BERTRAND RUSSELL

Cheerfulness and content
are great beautifiers, and
are famous preservers of
youthful looks.

CHARLES DICKENS

*F*lowers have a mysterious

and subtle influence upon

the feelings, not unlike some

strains of music. They relax

the tenseness of the mind.

HENRY WARD BEECHER

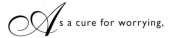 s a cure for worrying,

work is better than whisky.

THOMAS EDISON

$\mathcal{F}$ar and away the best prize that life offers

is the chance to work hard at work worth doing.

THEODORE ROOSEVELT

*B*e intent upon

the perfection of

the present day.

WILLIAM LAW

True silence is the rest of

the mind; it is to the spirit what

sleep is to the body, nourishment

and refreshment.

WILLIAM PENN

$\mathcal{I}$t is when we truly know and understand that we have a

limited time on earth, and that we have no way of knowing

when our time is up, that we will begin to live each day to the

fullest, as if it was the only one we had.

ELISABETH KUBLER-ROSS

$\mathcal{N}$othing contributes so much to

tranquillising the mind as a steady purpose.

MARY WOLLSTONECRAFT

Only those who have learned the power of sincere and selfless

contribution experience life's deepest joy: true fulfilment.

*U*ntil you make peace with

who you are, you'll never be

content with what you have.

DORIS MORTMAN

*W*ork is not always required. There is such

a thing as sacred idleness, the cultivation of

which is now fearfully neglected.

GEORGE MACDONALD

You do not need to leave your room.

Remain sitting at your table and listen.

Do not even listen, simply wait. Do not even

wait, be quite still and solitary. The world

will freely offer itself to you to be unmasked.

FRANZ KAFKA

He that knows how to go

out to some good purpose

and come back in peace can

be said to know the secret of

happy and successful living.

ANONYMOUS

he cure for all the illness of life is stored in the inner depth of life

itself, the access to which becomes possible when we are alone.

RABINDRANATH TAGORE

$\mathcal{S}$ometime in your life you will go on a journey. It will be the longest

journey you have ever taken. It is the journey to find yourself.

KATHERINE SHARP

$\mathscr{T}$here is no companion so

companionable as Solitude.

HENRY DAVID THOREAU

To sit in the shade on a fine day

is the most perfect refreshment.

JANE AUSTEN

Published in England by

FOUR SEASONS
PUBLISHING

16 Orchard Rise, Kingston upon Thames, Surrey, KT2 7EY

Designed in association with
THE BRIDGEWATER BOOK COMPANY

Printed in Singapore

Text selected by Pauline Barrett

The publishers would like to thank Gettyone Stone Picture Library for the use of pictures.

Copyright © 2000 Four Seasons Publishing Ltd

ISBN 1 85645 545 9